Joey's Journey

WHO RESCUED WHO?

By Kirk Montgomery

Illustrated By Moosa Habib

Curious Adventures Publishing
Colorado, U.S.A

Curious Adventures Publishing
An imprint of Journey Institute Press,
a division of 50 in 52 Journey, Inc.
journeyinstitutepress.org

Library of Congress Control Number: 2024950420
Names: Montgomery, Kirk
Title: Joey's Journey
Description: Colorado: Curious Adventures Publishing, 2024

Identifiers: ISBN 978-1-964754-20-8 (hardcover)
978-1-964754-21-5 (paperback)
978-1-964754-22-2 (ebook/kindle)
Subjects: BISAC:
JUVENILE NONFICTION / Animals / Dogs
JUVENILE NONFICTION / Animals / Animal Welfare
JUVENILE NONFICTION / Family / Adoption

First Edition
Printed in the United States of America

1 7 15 29 30 38 48 59 77 93

This book was typeset in Minion Pro

Cover Design by WiggleB Studios

For Joey 2007 - 2020

FOREWORD

A television newsroom is filled with "big" personalities. Inquisitive, creative, persistent people who work together to tell the stories of people in their community and beyond. A newsroom is lot like a family, we don't always get along, but we lean on each other when we are struggling.

When Kirk joined our newsroom, he made our family better. He brought us joy, light and lots of laughter. He wasn't just funny, he was kind and sensitive too. Even so, his huge heart had room to grow. He didn't know that, until he met Joey.

We watched Kirk's world change when Joey found him. He built his life around his new, forever friend. He told us funny stories about Joey, when he got a little mischievous, but also how he comforted him when he really needed a friend. Joey made Kirk a better man. He gave him new purpose too.

Kirk's "big" personality, made him a "big" deal in Denver. Viewers loved watching him. And they loved to hear about his little Joey. Kirk used his voice to help others find their own best friend. Kirk and Joey became famous. And like many famous duos, they gave us lots of unforgettable memories. Most of all, they taught us about unconditional love and how it comes to us in unexpected ways.

Kim Christiansen
Anchor - 9News | KUSA-TV

Hi, I'm Joey! My journey started in a shelter for stray animals in Denver, Colorado. I was very little, and I waited there for someone to pick me.

One day, I was taken to a TV station for something called Adopt-a-Pet. That's when I met Kirk, a friendly human behind a big desk. It had lots of lights and big robot looking things called "TV Camera's"

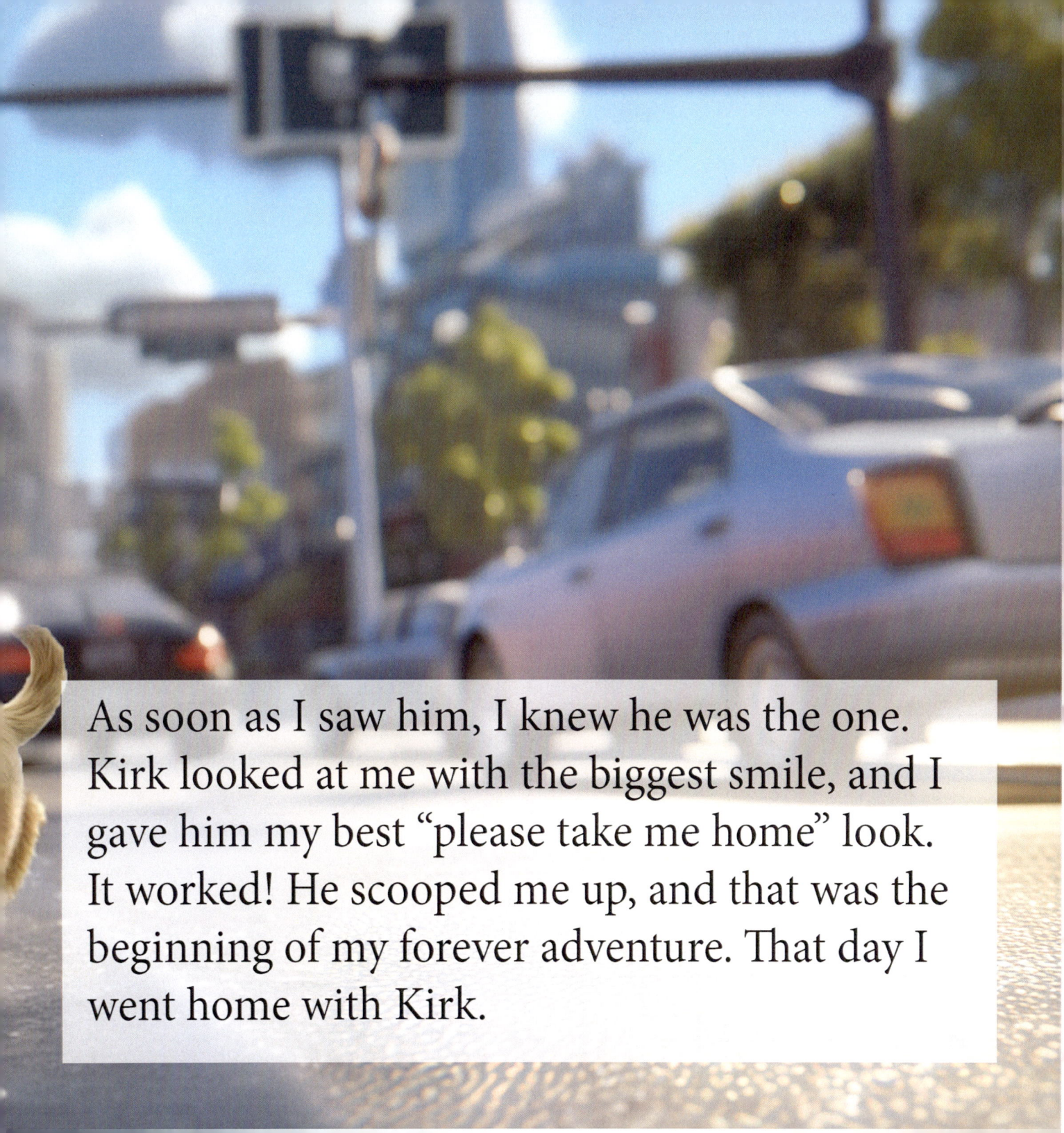

As soon as I saw him, I knew he was the one. Kirk looked at me with the biggest smile, and I gave him my best "please take me home" look. It worked! He scooped me up, and that was the beginning of my forever adventure. That day I went home with Kirk.

I was a little nervous. So nervous, in fact, that I had an accident in the car on the drive home. I'm sorry to say I made a big mess! Kirk had to pull over on the busy highway. We were only a few miles from the shelter, and I bet he was thinking that maybe he should take me back.

But Kirk didn't get mad. Instead, he cleaned me off, and said "Ok, kid. Let's get you home". That's when I realized I was exactly where I was meant to be.

My first adventure with Kirk was at a dog park! He let me off my leash, and I ran as fast as I could. I chased squirrels, sniffed every tree, and ran back to Kirk for belly rubs. What a day!

As time went on, Kirk and I grew closer. We went everywhere together. He'd talk about me on TV. Soon, I even got to be on my own show with him every week!

The show was called "Joey's Friends." People would come up to Kirk and me on walks just to say, "Hi, Joey!" I felt famous!

Kirk would talk about our adventures on TV. He'd share all the silly things I did, and the people watching loved it! I was pretty much a star.

Everywhere we went, I met lots of new friends. I loved playing with other dogs and humans. Everyone seemed to know me from my TV show.

The attention made me feel special. I loved how Kirk would gush about me. He would also talk about the importance of adopting from a shelter.

Kirk and I loved exploring together. One day, we moved from Denver to Kirk's hometown in Michigan. There, I made new friends!

At my new home, my favorite spot was by the window. I'd sit there watching and waiting for Kirk to come home. I would get so excited when he walked in the door! I knew I was safe, happy, and loved.

I loved my chew toys! Kirk would surprise me sometimes by bringing a new one home. And I loved anything that smelled like Kirk because it reminded me of him!

One day, he wasn't happy that I chewed up a toy that had his scent all over it. "Eyeglasses," I think he called it. Then he said I was a scamp!

No matter where Kirk went, I was right there with him. Whether he was working or relaxing, I stayed by his side, always ready for our next adventure.

Whenever Kirk was sad, I'd snuggle up beside him. I wanted him to know I was there, and I'd do anything to make him feel better. That's what best friends do.

My life with Kirk was full of love, laughter, and adventure. Every day was special, and I couldn't have asked for a better human to share my journey with.

Every day, I was so thankful that Kirk had rescued me. But I was confused sometimes when he would tell me that I had rescued him! He told me how much I had changed his life for the better.

As I got older, I slowed down a bit. My legs weren't as fast, and I took longer naps. But I never stopped loving my time with Kirk. And I knew he loved me too.

When I was thirteen, it was time for me to cross the Rainbow Bridge.
It was peaceful, and I knew Kirk was with me in spirit, just like he'd always been.

Even though I can no longer cuddle and play with Kirk, I know he remembers me every day. I was his best friend, and he was mine. I'll always be with him in his heart.

Kirk shared my story with so many people, and I hope it inspired others to adopt dogs like me. There are so many shelter pets waiting for their forever humans.

After I crossed the Rainbow Bridge, Kirk was sad for a long time. So I sent a new friend to Kirk from another shelter—a cat named Denver! Can you believe it?

Denver was named after the city where Kirk and I met. I know they'll have their own amazing adventures.

My journey with Kirk was full of love, and I'm so happy knowing Denver's will be as well.

The End

Special Thanks

To Jessica Roe for her hours of advice both technical and creative. To Michael Jenet for believing in this project and his endless patience. To my early readers : Ann Emmerich, Denise Pritchard, Eden Lane, Paula Woodward, Leslie Hart Davidson, John K Addis, and Jim Yanchus, thank you for your thoughtful and important input. To my Father and Brother Archie Stewart, and Kevin Stewart for all of the support... always. To Kim Christiansen for the beautiful memories and tear launching words, I miss you. To Wendy White, Cindy Scheopner, and Karen Shain, for putting their money where their mouth is. To Julie Flynn for the persistence that paid off. To Pam Grier, thank you for all of the love and support over the years. To Ginny Makita for her grace and compassion helping Joey cross the Rainbow Bridge, and to the Larimer County Humane Society, and Michele's Rescue for all the great work they do in finding forever homes for countless animals and for being the place I found my guys.

A note from Pam Grier

I've had to stop several times reading your glorious narrative of you and Joey. What a lovely story that should convince anyone to Find their "Joey," in my case my 11 Joeys!

My "Joeys" Lola, Zoe, Toto and Rudi keep me so safe and warm during winters and remind us all how lucky we are to have supported Rescue and adoptive organizations all over the country. In Native American culture, "Save a life, gain a life." Joey is watching over you everyday, Kirkie!

And Found Denver the cat for you!

Big hugs, and congratulations on your lovely book of Joey!

Pam Grier - **Actress**

About the Author

Kirk Montgomery is a multi-award-winning Journalist. He is also a still photographer and pet lover, who advocates the adoption of animals from rescue shelters. He lives in the Detroit area with his adopted cat "Denver". Joey's Journey is his first book.